smart com•pas•sion

\\ˈsmärt kəm-ˈpa-shən\\

▶ a handbook for making a difference
when you don't know where to start

wesley furlong

Herald Press
Harrisonburg, Virginia

Based on *Smart Compassion: How to Stop "Doing Outreach" and Start Making Change* by Wesley Furlong

SMART COMPASSION HANDBOOK
© 2017 by Herald Press, Harrisonburg, Virginia 22802. 800-245-7894.
International Standard Book Number: 978-1-5138-0180-3
Printed in United States of America
Cover and interior design by Reuben Graham

21 20 19 18 17   10 9 8 7 6 5 4 3 2 1

Contents

Introduction

What story does God want to write in your community?

What story is God already writing?

And how can you and others join that story?

This handbook is best read as part of a local conversation about your community's flourishing. It is designed to be used alongside *Smart Compassion: How to Stop "Doing Outreach" and Start Making Change* (Herald Press). Gather a group of people from your congregation or neighborhood or ministry team and find at least six times that you can meet together.

As you pray and live into a vision of God's kingdom in your community, what should you expect to change? What do you sense God doing in this season? What role are you to play in God's story? Such questions are best engaged in community, among people who are praying together and actively engaged in spending themselves well (see Isaiah 58:10).

The biblical concept of *shalom*, often translated as "peace," is far more than the absence of violence. It is the restoration of order and the fulfillment of purpose. "It is as it should be." In the creation story, after God creates the world, God steps back and calls it good. As you look around your community, on a micro, mezzo, and macro level, how does it look? What do you see? Where is it *not* as it should be? We need a God-inspired community imagination to overlie our view of present reality, and we need to pray and live into their convergence.

On a micro level, we embody *healing presence*. We hope for individuals to experience God's fullness of life in new ways. Our hopes and prayers can lead to sharing the gospel, or serving as a conduit of God's healing presence with someone, or both. On a mezzo level, we pursue *radical hospitality*, in which we extend our lives and homes to an individual or family. In our homes and within our neighborhoods, we intentionally seek to love people as Jesus loves us. On a macro level, we pursue *collective empowerment*. We long for and pursue a broader vision of justice, equity, and opportunity for those who are marginalized and oppressed.

Taken together, *Smart Compassion* and this handbook are intended to expand the conversation on community flourishing by introducing inspiring stories and best practices. I pray that these resources can help you and others in your church or small group or ministry team focus the conversation on your local context by providing practical frameworks and helpful tools.

My hope for this handbook is threefold:

1. That your intimacy with Christ grows and your faith is strengthened.

2. That your level of expectation to see God's shalom expand in your community rises.

3. That your level of clarity on where to start and what's most important grows.

Let me share a few ideas about how such hopes could be realized.

Encourage the experiential elements between sessions. Each session includes opportunities for journaling and going deeper. They'll make your times together much richer.

Keep prayer and God's Word central to both your times apart and your times together. Think about some ways to strengthen intercessory prayer in the group, for each other and your community. Either in the group or one-on-one, discuss spiritual formation practices and help those who might need assistance in establishing them.

Be honest, encourage appropriate degrees of transparency, and avoid pretense at all cost. It's far better to confess, "I struggle with apathy in this area" or "I don't think our family system is ready to invest that much right now," than it is to speak on merely an abstract level or with half-truths.

Where possible, move beyond good intentions to plans that include accountability. Even if the vision or intention is to pursue greater discernment in an area, it's a helpful practice to move our words into action plans.

Make sure to process potential next steps as a group at the end of study. The "Where Do We Go from Here?" section of this handbook (pp. 73–79) is designed to help you process and prepare for next steps. If individuals in your group were unable to complete some of the Go Deeper exercises (such as the ACE test or Gifts Assessment), you may want to spend some time working through them before moving forward, since they are referenced in the "Roadmap for Community Engagement."

What else would you add? What are your hopes? How can they be realized? Spend some time in prayer and ask God to help you see the new life he is calling forward.

As you move forward, may God ground and root you deep in his love, and may his love overflow into your relationships. May he fill you to full measure with his grace, and may the fruits and gifts of the Holy Spirit manifest in new and surprising ways in your life.

Please share with me your experience in your community. Connect with me at WesleyFurlong.com. I would love to hear from you!

—*Wesley Furlong*

How to Use This Study Guide

This handbook is one part conversation guide and one part field guide. The six sessions follow the overall flow of the book and include elements such as Pray, Ask, Begin, Read Scripture, Study, and Discuss. Each session also includes several opportunities for further engagement. The sessions engage chapters from *Smart Compassion* (usually two or three chapters per session) but primarily consist of new content that aims to bridge concepts in the book with contextual and practical questions. For instance, chapter 4 in *Smart Compassion* ("A Love Differentiated") and chapter 8 ("Boundaries and Your Capacity for Chaos") are both referenced in session 4 of this handbook ("Boundary-Shifting Love"). The session builds on concepts in the two chapters by exploring the tension between hospitality and boundaries in greater depth and by recommending specific exercises for application.

It is ideal if group members read the related chapters in *Smart Compassion* before your group meets. If you are the leader, encourage your group members to find time to at least skim the chapters before the session—even as you recognize that schedules may sometimes prevent individuals from doing so. Hopefully you can use the group time to pray together, to discuss interpretation and application of the Scripture and concepts, and to identify key action-oriented takeaways and next steps.

Allow the study and discussion sections to serve as guides, but do not feel confined to them. It might be helpful, toward the end of the gatherings, to highlight the potential next steps and allow individuals to share their practical takeaways. You might also want to organize a closed Facebook or other social media group to upload additional content and facilitate group conversation between meetings. In the back of this handbook, you will find a list of resources and suggested next steps for further study and practical engagement.

Session 1

What Should We Expect?

▶ Imagine God's kingdom in your community

Pray

Share prayer concerns and praises from the past week. Pray this prayer together:

Father, unveil our eyes to see our community as you see it. We want to do what we see you doing. Give us the discernment and faith to align our yeses and nos to your Word. Amen.

Ask

Close your eyes and imagine what the community around your church looks like as God's kingdom takes deeper root and begins to expand across the region. What do you see?

If possible, read chapter 1 of *Smart Compassion* before this session.

Begin

In 1970, a small group of students with quadriplegia attending the University of California grew tired of having their classes located down a hill and then having to ask for help to push their wheelchairs back uphill. Navigating roads was difficult and dangerous given the high curbs of the sidewalks, so they would use driveways or loading docks to access the busy streets and roll to the next driveway. One night, the students decided to pour a crude sidewalk ramp that would enable them to cross a busy campus street. Soon, curb cuts—sidewalk ramps—started popping up in other cities. Today, these small ramps in sidewalks are a basic part of pedestrian crossings that enable people with disabilities to safely cross streets.

What started as an act of imagination and courage—arising from the belief that "It shouldn't be this way"—is now a given in cities today.

The act of imagining and living into a vision of God's kingdom in our communities is our first topic of conversation. In the Old Testament, the word *shalom* (most often translated "peace") embodied more than an absence of violence. It was the presence of life as God intended. There's much we can look at around us and think, "It's not supposed to be this way."

How can we respond to the gap in our communities between what *is* and what *should be?*

Read Scripture

Zechariah 4:1-10

Then the angel who talked with me returned and woke me up, like someone awakened from sleep. He asked me, "What do you see?"

I answered, "I see a solid gold lampstand with a bowl at the top and seven lamps on it, with seven channels to the lamps. Also there are two olive trees by it, one on the right of the bowl and the other on its left."

I asked the angel who talked with me, "What are these, my lord?"

He answered, "Do you not know what these are?"

"No, my lord," I replied.

So he said to me, "This is the word of the Lord to Zerubbabel: 'Not by might nor by power, but by my Spirit,' says the Lord Almighty.

"What are you, mighty mountain? Before Zerubbabel you will become level ground. Then he will bring out the capstone to shouts of 'God bless it! God bless it!'"

Then the word of the Lord came to me: "The hands of Zerubbabel have laid the foundation of this temple; his hands will also complete it. Then you will know that the Lord Almighty has sent me to you.

"Who dares despise the day of small things, since the seven eyes of the Lord that range throughout the earth will rejoice when they see the chosen capstone in the hand of Zerubbabel?"

Study

The angel's question—"What do you see?"—is important. For the prophet, the most likely answer was "disappointment." The foundation for the new temple had been laid sixteen years before this moment, and it served as an ever-present reminder of unrealized dreams. Proverbs 13:12 says, "Hope deferred makes the heart sick." When the angel asked this question, the hearts of the people of Israel were sick. I imagine the prophet responding, "Well, I see a temple that was never built, a shortage of workers, a lack of resources, and a lot of hostile people in every direction." Sound familiar?

The angel then gave this stunning revelation: a solid gold lampstand with seven lamps between two olive trees. An endless supply of light and power! There were signs of decay in every direction, but God gave the prophet a beautiful revelation of new life that he simply couldn't imagine. What Zechariah saw: a mountain that had to be quarried, by people who weren't there, with tools they couldn't afford, for a temple that no one in the area wanted to see built. What God saw: wholeness, flourishing, salvation, and shalom!

Our need for control and understanding can become unnecessary ceilings that limit God's work in our lives. Jesus said, "If you have faith as small as a mustard seed, you can say to this mountain, 'Move from here to there,' and it will move. Nothing will be impossible for you" (Matthew 17:20). In the opening verses of Zechariah 4, the angel shifted the prophet's focus from the obstacles and deficits to a new, God-given vision for Israel. "Who dares despise the day of small things?" the angel asked.

Four years later, the temple was finished. Somehow, the people showed up. Somehow, the mountain was quarried and the enemies were held back. And then, one weekend, God's people had a party they never thought they'd experience in a million years.

It's always this way: Decay sets in. People get discouraged, retreat, and give their lives to lesser visions. But when God breaks in, he shares a crazy vision that is far beyond the capacity of people to attain it. The work starts small—sometimes excruciatingly small—with people who set aside their own agendas to pursue God's vision. Resistance is encountered, and faith is tested. Eventually, reality itself starts to change. Hudson Taylor captured it well: "God's work done God's way will never lack God's supply."

Smart compassion is the full pursuit of a community's flourishing in a spirit of worship and prayer. Smart compassion holds together justice and evangelism, wisdom and revelation, and the broadly communal and deeply personal aspects of life. Smart compassion learns from a Nobel laureate's research on the return on investment of early childhood education and uses trustworthy data to measure effectiveness. It rejects the toxic "giver" and "receiver" posture of disempowering aid and starts from a strengths-based perspective. First and foremost, it never loses sight of Jesus as the Giver, Sustainer, and Redeemer of life and strives to maintain his posture in John 5:19: "I do what I see the Father doing."

—*Smart Compassion*, p. 10

Discuss

▶ Name some modern examples of the themes in this Scripture passage. Share personal examples of these themes.

▶ How does our need for control become an unnecessary ceiling that limits God's work in our lives? What are ways you sometimes limit God's work in your life?

▶ It's easy to become overwhelmed by the needs and opportunities around us. How are we to respond to the gap between what *is* in our communities and what *should be*?

▶ How do we avoid becoming anesthetized to the suffering of others?

▶ How can you and your congregation cultivate the wisdom and imagination to wage peace in pursuit of God's shalom?

▶ What are some tangible ways you can envision engaging in smart compassion right now?

Journal

Sit before the Lord this week with the question, "What do you see?" Ask God to unveil your eyes to the new things he is doing in your community and the parts where you're invited to collaborate. Try to maintain a posture of expectant receptivity to the Lord as you go through familiar rhythms.

Go Deeper

Use the QR code at the bottom of this page or go to Refuge.life and click on "Learn" and then "Map Your Community." Here are some questions to consider as you look at the links and see what you can find out about your community.

- ► How many households in your community live below the poverty line?

- ► How does your county's access to primary and mental healthcare compare to other counties in the state?

- ► How many children in foster care are available for adoption?

Session 2

The Posture of Compassion

▶ Get comfortable with suffering

Pray

Share prayer concerns and praises from the past week and pray together.

> *Father, let me learn by paradox that the way down is the way up, that to be low is to be high, that the broken heart is the healed heart, that the contrite spirit is the rejoicing spirit, that the repenting soul is the victorious soul, that to have nothing is to possess all, that to bear the cross is to wear the crown, that to give is to receive, that the valley is the place of vision. . . . Let me find your light in my darkness, your life in my death, your joy in my sorrow, your grace in my sin, your riches in my poverty, your glory in my valley.*

> —The Valley of Vision: A Collection of Puritan Prayers and Devotions

Ask

Think of a time that you walked with someone through a difficult time in life. How comfortable are you in "sitting on the ash heap" with someone who is suffering?

If possible, read chapter 2 of *Smart Compassion* before this session.

Begin

The first work of smart compassion is connecting with others in their suffering. But you can't do that unless you've learned to suffer well yourself.

Compassion means to "suffer with" another person. In her novel *To Kill a Mockingbird*, Harper Lee captures the posture of compassion well: "You never really understand a person until you consider things from his point of view . . . until you climb into his skin and walk around in it."

The posture of compassion requires *proximity* and *solidarity.* We get up close to the person who is suffering (proximity), and we meet that person on level ground (solidarity) instead of imagining that we're reaching down to him or her. Compassion also requires *emotional connectedness*: being deeply connected to another's perspective and feelings.

In this session, we distinguish compassion from other types of service and recognize its unique gift and capacity to bring life even in places of death.

Read Scripture

2 Corinthians 1:3-4

Praise be to the God and Father of our Lord Jesus Christ, the Father of compassion and the God of all comfort, who comforts us in all our troubles, so that we can comfort those in any trouble with the comfort we ourselves receive from God.

Romans 5:3-4

Not only so, but we also glory in our sufferings, because we know that suffering produces perseverance; perseverance, character; and character, hope.

Study

The word *paraclete*, which is translated "comforter," occurs five times in 2 Corinthians 1:4. The Paraclete is personified as the Holy Spirit and includes the imagery of "one who walks beside us." Follow the apostle Paul's train of thought in this opening greeting to the church: "Praise be to . . . the Father of compassion and our Paraclete" (verse 3), "who comforts us in our troubles" (verse 4).

Let's pause here for a moment. The word translated "trouble," *thlipsis*, means "pressure" or "pressing." Elsewhere in the apostle Paul's writings, this word is translated as "suffering." *Thlipsis* described the act of squeezing olives in a press in order to extract the oil. During the first century, it was also a Roman torture technique, in which a large boulder was placed on someone's chest until she or he suffocated.

When you squeeze something, what comes out is what is inside. Martin Luther wrote, "Whatever [virtues] tribulation finds us in, it develops more fully. If anyone is carnal, weak, blind, wicked, irascible, haughty, and so forth, tribulation will make him [or her] more carnal, weak, blind, wicked and irritable. On the other hand, if one is spiritual, strong, wise, pious, gentle and humble, he [or she] will become more spiritual, powerful, wise, pious, gentle and humble."1

In Romans 5:3-4, the apostle Paul writes, "We also glory in our sufferings [*thlipsis*], because we know that suffering [*thlipsis*] produces perseverance; perseverance, character; and character, hope."

In the brief verses from the 2 Corinthians passage, Paul explains how this is possible. Verse 4 opens with

---

1. Martin Luther, *Commentary on Romans* 2nd ed. (Grand Rapids, MI: Zondervan, 1976), 90–91.

the recognition of God's sovereign presence with us amid suffering and adversity. The next part of the verse begins with an all-important "so that," where our role changes in relationship to suffering and comfort: "So that we can be *paraclete* with those in any *thlipsis.*"

We move from being the *recipients* of comfort to the *conduits* of comfort. And to reinforce the relational and spiritual dimension of comfort here, Paul bookends it with the phrase "with the *paraclete-ness* we ourselves receive from God, our *Paraclete.*"

God, in all his sovereignty and goodness, walks with us through *thlipsis* so that we can walk with others through *thlipsis* with the very presence and power that God has given us!

The posture of compassion requires long-suffering in uncomfortable places. You have to create a safe place for authenticity. Brad affirmed what he could and sat with me as I talked in circles. He was smart: he didn't feed into my warped perspective by saying, "Yeah, you're right. That's awful. Let me pat you on the back as you plunge headlong over that cliff." He also never asked questions like, "What are your deepest desires?" But he was compassionate, so neither did he cut me off with, "You just need to go back and fix this right now." He affirmed what he could and didn't validate my accusations or bitterness. Instead, after listening to my long diatribe of accusations and judgments, Brad said, "It's hard to forgive, isn't it?" There was authenticity in his empathy. But the focus on forgiveness oriented me toward life.

—*Smart Compassion*, p. 39

Discuss

▶ Discuss the redemptive nature of suffering. What does that phrase mean? Where have you experienced God's redeeming grace in your life?

▶ How comfortable are you in sitting on the ash heap with someone who is suffering?

▶ Discuss the idea of being a conduit of God's presence. What might that include beyond acts of kindness or empathy?

▶ Look at the "Giving postures" graphic on page 75 in the Resources section. Discuss the five different postures outlined in that graphic and the questions it contains.

▶ Imagine and discuss this scenario: A small group from your church wants to help a struggling neighborhood a couple of miles away. The neighborhood has a high concentration of poverty and crime. The group tosses around some ideas for service but can't settle on anything specific. So they decide to interview people in a public housing community. After introducing themselves, members of the small group say, "We're looking to get involved in the community and are curious if there's something we can do to help. Do you have any specific needs we might be able to meet or know of areas where we should get involved?" Some residents are polite and affirm their desire to help the community. But most people express frustration at the church group's presumptuous questions.

▷ Why might residents have been frustrated with the group's approach?

▷ If a member of the small group told you about this initial experience and asked, "What should we do differently?" how would you respond?

▷ What would a posture of compassion look like in such a scenario?

Here's an absolutely extraordinary thought that becomes an even more extraordinary reality when we experience it: we can become conduits of God's very presence and power to others.

—*Smart Compassion*, p. 36

Journal

Reflect on 2 Corinthians 1:3-4 and Romans 5:3-4. Ask the Lord to identify areas and people with whom you can embody a posture of compassion. What are some personal experiences of your own that carry the "so that" potential of the 2 Corinthians passage? What experiences in your life enable you to now serve as a conduit of God's redemptive grace?

☀ Go Deeper

▶ Practice listening well to people this week. Try to eliminate hurry and mental preoccupation so that you can be more fully present to people.

▶ Identify where and with whom you can begin to embody the posture of compassion in more intentional ways.

▶ Take the ACE test (an assessment of adverse childhood experiences) via the QR code. Become familiar with the ACE Study and the implications of the prevalence of trauma and the relationship between biography and biology.

Session 3

The Gift of Attention

▶ Cultivate intimacy with God and be ready for divine appointments

Pray

Share prayer concerns and praises from the past week and pray together.

> *Father, help us to be fully present to you and the people around us this week. Free us from the bondage to our schedules so that we are free to respond to your nudge and your call.*

Ask

How do you cultivate intimacy with God in your daily rhythms of life? What ways have you found to listen to God throughout your day?

If possible, read chapters 3, 5, and 6 of *Smart Compassion* before this session.

Begin

At the start of the day, many of us have a certain number of appointments on our calendars. With our task lists, we have a reasonable sense of what the day will hold. *Chronos* is the Greek word for this kind of calendar time: it's the time we live in, the time we measure with days and hours and minutes and that we fill with meetings and appointments.

Kairos is another Greek word for time, but this word conveys the idea of a divine appointment—a kind of "timeless time" in which we respond to God's timing and call and in which we experience the presence of God. When we begin to recognize God's presence in our daily lives and respond to the unexpected divine appointments that God opens for us, the background of life suddenly moves into the foreground.

Our focus in this session is on cultivating intimacy with God in our daily rhythms and responding to potential *kairos* moments. We may schedule our *chronos* time, but we are to hold our schedules with open hands. We can expect *kairos* to break into the *chronos*—the sacred to fuse with the mundane.

Time management trainings and a myriad of books and seminars on productivity had instilled in me a relentless need to concentrate on what was most important. It wasn't easy, but I had learned to block out my surroundings and concentrate my attention. But was the virtue now a vice? Had I taken the pursuit of concentration too far?

—**Smart Compassion, p. 48**

Read Scripture

Acts 8:26-40

Now an angel of the Lord said to Philip, "Go south to the road—the desert road—that goes down from Jerusalem to Gaza." So he started out, and on his way he met an Ethiopian eunuch, an important official in charge of all the treasury of the Kandake (which means "queen of the Ethiopians"). This man had gone to Jerusalem to worship, and on his way home was sitting in his chariot reading the Book of Isaiah the prophet. The Spirit told Philip, "Go to that chariot and stay near it."

Then Philip ran up to the chariot and heard the man reading Isaiah the prophet. "Do you understand what you are reading?" Philip asked.

"How can I," he said, "unless someone explains it to me?" So he invited Philip to come up and sit with him.

This is the passage of Scripture the eunuch was reading:

"He was led like a sheep to the slaughter,

and as a lamb before its shearer is silent,

so he did not open his mouth.

In his humiliation he was deprived of justice.

Who can speak of his descendants?

For his life was taken from the earth."

The eunuch asked Philip, "Tell me, please, who is the prophet talking about, himself or someone else?" Then Philip began with that very passage of Scripture and told him the good news about Jesus.

As they traveled along the road, they came to some water and the eunuch said, "Look, here is water. What can stand in the way of my being baptized?" And he gave orders to stop the chariot. Then both Philip and the eunuch went down into the water and Philip bap-tized him. When they came up out of the water, the Spirit of the Lord suddenly took Philip away, and the eunuch did not see him again, but went on his way re-joicing. Philip, however, appeared at Azotus and trav-eled about, preaching the gospel in all the towns until he reached Caesarea.

Listening well, in ways that communicate accep-tance and fully attend to the heart, opens the pathways for a healing presence.

—Smart Compassion, p. 71

Study

This passage tells the story of a divine appointment—of someone who was so in tune with God that he showed up just where and when he was supposed to be. In verse 26, an angel of God said to Philip, "Go"—or in some translations, "Rise and go" (ESV). In the next verse, we hear that Philip "started out"—or "rose and went" (ESV). These two verses capture the essence of our greatest human potential: to walk fully receptive and obedient to God's voice regardless of how well it aligns with our expectations, desires, history, rationality, or resources. Philip simply said yes to God's yes, even when it led him to a desert road. He responded to the angel the same way Mary did after the improbable announcement of Jesus' birth: "Let it be to me according to your word" (Luke 1:38 ESV).

We aren't given any indication that Philip vocalized the hundred "But what about . . ." questions that must have flooded his mind in the moment. Even if he thought those, it is clear that he didn't allow them to serve as a filter for what God was free to do in and through his life.

When we maintain a posture that says, "God, help us to be fully present to you and the people around us," our perspective changes. Even the best of our personal pursuits for achievement begin to feel a bit vacuous compared to life lived *coram Deo*: before the face of God.

May we each get to the same place of full receptivity and obedience to the voice of God that Philip found. May God give us strength to respond to the unexpected opportunities he invites us to pursue.

Discuss

▶ What are some personal obstacles that hinder you from recognizing and responding to potential *kairos* moments?

▶ Eliminating hurry and mental preoccupation and embracing inconveniences are essential aspects of responding to divine appointments. How can we cultivate these practices with greater intentionality?

▶ With what activities or commitments are you most tempted to replace intimacy with God? What are the primary pursuits that threaten your attentiveness to God's call?

▶ What is the difference between hearing someone's voice and actually listening to that person?

▶ Discuss your personal challenges to practicing undistracted and nonjudgmental listening.

▶ How do you hold in tension the need for concentration and goals and the need to be fully present and open to unexpected opportunities?

▶ What are some morning practices that might help you prepare for going through the day fully present to God and people?

Undistracted and nonjudgmental listening doesn't necessitate a whitewashing of truth. It builds and preserves the relational bridge required for truth to cross.

—Smart Compassion, p. 65

Journal

Review the Go Deeper section. Reflect on the nudging you experienced. What were the potential opportunities you sensed? How did you respond? Are you listening more attentively? Are you finding ways to express love more tangibly? Have you noticed a higher degree of contentment, joy, or hope?

Go Deeper

▶ Begin each morning this week with the following prayer: *God, help me to see where you're at work. Help me to love, listen, discern, and respond.* When you sense a small prompting to initiate something unexpected—for example, a conversation or an act of service—don't dismiss it. Respond to the prompting, even if you're not 100 percent sure that it is from God.

▶ End each evening with a short journal entry of your experience (see the Journal section on the previous page).

▶ Watch the Time to Revive video "How to Share the Gospel" using the QR code.

▶ What is the relationship between justice and evangelism? Reflect on the "Ways to approach evangelism and justice" graphic on page 73 in the Resources section. Which number reflects your congregation's approach to community engagement? Read the following Scriptures and reflect on how your worldview influences your community engagement practices:

Psalm 85:10-11	Luke 4:18-19
Amos 5:24	Luke 17:20-21
Micah 6:8	John 18:36
Isaiah 58:5-12	Acts 28:31
Matthew 6:9-13	Revelation 11:15
Matthew 25:31-46	Revelation 21:3-4
Matthew 28:18-20	

Session 4

Boundary-Shifting Love

▶ Grow in love, hospitality, and wisdom

Pray

Share prayer concerns and praises from the past week.

Pray this prayer together:

Lord, make me an instrument of thy peace. Where there is hatred, let me sow love; where there is injury, pardon; where there is doubt, faith; where there is despair, hope; where there is darkness, light; where there is sadness, joy.

O divine Master, grant that I may not so much seek to be consoled as to console; to be understood as to understand; to be loved as to love. For it is in giving that we receive; it is in pardoning that we are pardoned; it is in dying to self that we are born to eternal life.

—Prayer of Saint Francis

Ask

Reflect back over your life and times that you were on the receiving end of hospitality. What did it feel like to be welcomed with open arms into someone else's home?

If possible, read chapters 4 and 8 of *Smart Compassion* before this session.

Begin

The word *hospitality* may make us think of fancy dinner parties or entertaining guests in lovely homes. But hospitality means embracing strangers as extended family. It means opening our lives and homes to others even when it is inconvenient or our house is messy. By its very nature, love expands our boundaries. It doesn't eviscerate them; it widens them. The reason we extend ourselves and our families and open our homes to strangers is that we love as Jesus loves. He set an example for us and said, "Do as I have done" (John 13:15) and "You will be blessed if you do" (John 13:17).

Yet in the same way that healthy parenting requires both appropriate boundaries and unconditional love, the wise extension of radical hospitality requires truth and love. When you're presented with a specific opportunity to practice radical hospitality, how do you determine the appropriate response? The very same boundaries can be established out of self-absorption or a clear sense of purpose. The very same openness to radical hospitality can come from deep deficits or deep love. What is the difference between this boundary-shifting love and becoming a doormat for anyone to walk over? The question of how to grow in love, hospitality, and wisdom is our focus in this session.

> When we live in the knowledge that we are in Christ, people and circumstances are not ultimately sovereign over our lives. God is sovereign. He is our Redeemer. God is able to affirm our identity, meet our needs, drive out our fears, and wash us of the effects of sin. As the apostle Paul writes, we are "being rooted and established in [God's] love" (Ephesians 3:17). When we are in Christ, we are able to cast our burdens on the Lord, and he keeps us in peace as we keep our eyes on him. The effect of our grounding in God's love is that we don't look to others to repay every debt they owe us. We forgive debts, just as we are forgiven. As we forgive, we bring the recipients face-to-face with unmerited grace.
>
> **—Smart Compassion, p. 61**

📖 Read Scripture

John 13:1-5

It was just before the Passover Festival. Jesus knew that the hour had come for him to leave this world and go to the Father. Having loved his own who were in the world, he loved them to the end.

The evening meal was in progress, and the devil had already prompted Judas, the son of Simon Iscariot, to betray Jesus. Jesus knew that the Father had put all things under his power, and that he had come from God and was returning to God; so he got up from the meal, took off his outer clothing, and wrapped a towel around his waist. After that, he poured water into a basin and began to wash his disciples' feet, drying them with the towel that was wrapped around him.

John 13:12-15

When he had finished washing their feet, he put on his clothes and returned to his place. "Do you understand what I have done for you?" he asked them. "You call me 'Teacher' and 'Lord,' and rightly so, for that is what I am. Now that I, your Lord and Teacher, have washed your feet, you also should wash one another's feet. I have set you an example that you should do as I have done for you.

John 13:34-35

A new command I give you: Love one another. As I have loved you, so you must love one another. By this everyone will know that you are my disciples, if you love one another.

Study

Betrayal to the point of death: this is the context for these words, which are introduced in a way unlike any other teaching in the gospel. This is the only time in the gospel that Jesus says, "Here's a new command." The command to love isn't new; what's different is the phrase "as I have loved you."

We are to love people not as they deserve or according to how we feel about them, but as Jesus loves us. We see Jesus wash the feet of the man who will betray him to the point of death and then say to the disciples, "Do as I have done for you." When they do this, Jesus says, everyone will know they are his disciples.

Jesus' example and teaching in John 13 preclude any situation where we can freely justify sidestepping love in the pursuit of truth. Given what we see in this passage, we can't say about our own modern-day experiences, "Well, this is a different situation. That guy *deserved* it!" or "Jesus loving everyone was great, but that just doesn't work in our lives now." When Jesus washes the feet of his betrayer, he commands us to follow his example. Period. Jesus extends this new commandment, and concludes by elevating it to the status of the greatest single indicator of our relationship with Jesus. Through watching Jesus in this scene, we recognize the completely otherworldly way of responding to unmet expectations, unjust suffering, and the people responsible for it.

Yet what about boundaries? Is there any place for them? Yes. When it comes to the tension between hospitality and boundaries, it's helpful to think about how tension produces growth. There's no growth without tension, but tension must be wisely calibrated. Somewhere between atrophy and being torn apart is a good stretching. Fully immersive experiences have their place, and every faith journey brings us to chasms where we jump or we don't jump. There are no baby steps across a chasm. But in general, growth is a process of being slowly and consistently stretched. Peter Senge, author of *The Fifth Discipline*, describes healthy tension with this metaphor: Imagine you hold your hands together, one on top of the other, and you place small rubber bands around each pair of fingers. As you pull your hands apart, you begin to feel the tension. There's no tension at a place of rest. But if you quickly pull your hands apart and rip off the rubber bands, you no longer have tension either. Tension must be wisely calibrated.

It's good and appropriate to wrestle with the tension between hospitality and boundaries. May God grant us the wisdom to do so.

You can think of this distinction between the source and object of our love in the light of philanthropy. A philanthropist draws a great deal of money from one source and chooses to give it freely to another source. The source and the recipient are clearly distinguished. In Jesus' new commandment, he does the same with the source and recipients of our love. We are to love people, not as they deserve or according to how we feel about them, but as Jesus has loved us. God is the source; people are the recipients.

—Smart Compassion, p. 61

Discuss

- ▶ What do you think Jesus would have said or done to Judas if he had seen him after his betrayal?

- ▶ Have you ever been a Judas—angry, guilty, and ashamed—and received unconditional love from someone else?

- ▶ Read 1 Corinthians 13. After the opening descriptions of love, the chapter describes childhood and adulthood. What is the connection of verse 11 to love? Discuss what difference it makes to distinguish the source and object of our love.

- ▶ When people are deeply rooted in God's transcendent love, it's a deeply spiritual reality. They are in love, as much as they are "in" any given circumstance, because they are in Christ. This phrase—"in Christ"—occurs ninety-two times in the New Testament. Discuss some practical examples of such love.

- ▶ In what ways can you begin to live out Jesus' new commandment to love as he loves us?

- ▶ Discuss areas where you feel tension between pursuing radical hospitality and healthy boundaries.

- ▶ Where do you think you should stretch toward greater hospitality?

- ▶ Where are the best and wisest opportunities to extend your family and open your home?

Journal

Reflect on these sentences: We can't say yes to everything, and it's important to get our yeses right. Every yes is ten thousand nos. Too many yeses is no yes. A half-hearted yes is a disguised no. A presumptuous yes is a no to the right yes.

Now reflect on your own yeses and nos. Are there yeses in your life that you sense God calling you to turn into nos? Are there nos you have said that God is prompting you to turn into yeses?

Go Deeper

▶ For a period of several days or weeks—twenty-one days works well—read 1 Corinthians 13:1-7 each morning. As you read, pray: *God, help these traits come alive in me today, especially where they're most tested.* At the end of the day, reread the Scripture as a prayer of self-examination. During this time, pay attention to times when you extend or receive forgiveness. Via the QR code, you can download a free ebook called *28 Days to Love* to serve as a guide for the journey.

▶ Identify areas where you can begin to grow into radical hospitality. Once you have clarity, develop a plan and enlist accountability.

▶ Read about the BREAD of radical hospitality on pages 101 and 105–17 of *Smart Compassion*. Identify practices that might help you cultivate hospitality in more intentional ways.

Session 5

Spend Yourself Well

▶ Align your beliefs and your actions

Pray

Share prayer concerns and praises from the past week.

Then pray this prayer together:

Father, you have my permission to rearrange anything that needs to be rearranged to accomplish your purposes. Please give me the wisdom and grace to align my will with your Word and your truth.

Ask

Where is the clearest intersection between your gifts and the needs that you perceive in your community?

If possible, read chapters 9, 10, and 11 of *Smart Compassion* before this session.

Begin

What explains the relationship between these three realities?

1. Most people recognize the dangers of texting while driving.

2. No one intends to cause an accident because of texting while driving.

3. Many accidents occur because people are texting while driving.

How does the "ping" of a text message lead us to do something we recognize as unwise? In the moment, the risks and rewards look different from when we view them abstractly. "It's just a short response, and I'm mostly looking at the road," we might say, or, "There's almost no chance this short text will cause an accident, and I'm pretty good at texting without looking."

This scenario illustrates the strengths and limitations of our will. If I recognize texting while driving as a temptation, it is far easier to make one single choice—download an app that prevents me from texting while driving—than it is to ignore texts every time they pop up. One decisive act is easier than needing to repeat a decision that conflicts with our desires.

Similarly, if I want to live a generous and compassionate life, it is easier to preselect the actions that best align with those values than it is to trust my will to choose wisely in the moment. For example, if generosity includes giving away a certain percentage of my time and money, it is better to identify a specific plan and implement it than it is to assume it will happen naturally.

When it comes to following Jesus' example and loving people as he loves us, it is easy for misalignment to occur between our values and actions. Our calendars, bank statements, and Internet search history might reveal a different set of values than what we *say* we espouse. This lesson is focused on how we can establish better alignment between our beliefs and our actions.

Read Scripture

Luke 16:1-13

> Jesus told his disciples: "There was a rich man whose manager was accused of wasting his possessions. So he called him in and asked him, 'What is this I hear about you? Give an account of your management, because you cannot be manager any longer.'
>
> "The manager said to himself, 'What shall I do now? My master is taking away my job. I'm not strong enough to dig, and I'm ashamed to beg—I know what

I'll do so that, when I lose my job here, people will welcome me into their houses.'

"So he called in each one of his master's debtors. He asked the first, 'How much do you owe my master?'

"'Nine hundred gallons of olive oil,' he replied.

"The manager told him, 'Take your bill, sit down quickly, and make it four hundred and fifty.'

"Then he asked the second, 'And how much do you owe?'

"'A thousand bushels of wheat,' he replied.

"He told him, 'Take your bill and make it eight hundred.'

"The master commended the dishonest manager because he had acted shrewdly. For the people of this world are more shrewd in dealing with their own kind than are the people of the light. I tell you, use worldly wealth to gain friends for yourselves, so that when it is gone, you will be welcomed into eternal dwellings.

"Whoever can be trusted with very little can also be trusted with much, and whoever is dishonest with very little will also be dishonest with much. So if you have not been trustworthy in handling worldly wealth, who will trust you with true riches? And if you have not been trustworthy with someone else's property, who will give you property of your own?

"No one can serve two masters. Either you will hate the one and love the other, or you will be devoted to the one and despise the other. You cannot serve both God and money."

Study

We might not have expected to hear these words from Jesus: "The master commended the dishonest manager because he had acted shrewdly. . . . I tell you, use worldly wealth to gain friends for yourselves" (verses 8-9). What? What is Jesus really saying here?

"Worldly wealth" simply means money. This parable aims to adjust our perspective on our time and money to an eternal viewpoint. The dishonest manager leveraged the small amount of time and resources he had for future gain. Jesus isn't suggesting we follow his specific behaviors. Instead, Jesus uses this story to invite us to reconsider how we see and think about our limited time and resources. We can leverage our small amount of time and resources for eternal purposes. A wise use of time and money keeps eternity in view at all times.

In the winter of 1938, Nicholas Winton was planning to travel to Switzerland for a ski vacation. He was a young stockbroker living in England, and he heard reports of Germany's likely incursion into Czechoslovakia. He canceled his ski trip and went to see if there was anything he could to do to help the children most likely to suffer, mostly Jewish children. Over the course of two years, Winton was able to rescue 669 children and bring them to England. For fifty years, little was known about his efforts. He had kept careful notes about the children (for example, their names and the addresses where they were placed), but never spoke about it. When his wife discovered the journals, attempts were made to follow up with the survivors. In 1988, Winton was a guest on the BBC television show *That's Life* to discuss the rescue attempts. What he didn't know was that the producers had filled the small auditorium with eighty of the people he had rescued. After hearing the story of the woman sitting next to Winton, the announcer said, "Is there anyone in our audience tonight who owes their life to Nicholas Winton? If so, could you stand up, please?" Dozens of people in the room stood up.

In this parable, Jesus leads us to imagine conversations like this in light of eternity, in which material stuff (money and possessions) and time are leveraged for truly significant purposes.

For followers of Jesus, an eternal worldview helps brings clarity to the practical questions about radical hospitality. When we shift our mind-set from the temporal to the eternal, our priorities shift with it. If God is sovereign, present, and actively at work in this world, redeeming his creation; if people are eternal beings with whom God longs to reconcile himself; and if we join God in his ministry of reconciliation, then eternity-changing opportunities are always before us! Our posture of being fully present to God and people opens the door to these opportunities for new life to flourish.

—Smart Compassion, p. 127

Discuss

▶ In what ways might an eternal perspective on life change the way you'll approach upcoming decisions?

▶ What are some practices that might help you maintain an eternal perspective on life?

▶ Where do you sense the need for greater alignment between personal values and actions in your life right now? What steps do you need to take to establish it?

Radical hospitality is one of the greatest gifts we can give our communities. We need individuals and families willing to move food pantries into their kitchens, put people first, risk vulnerability, leave space, and anticipate *kairos* moments with eager expectancy. It's a countercultural way to live, but it's also part of the basic package of following Jesus. We extend hospitality to strangers, heal the sick, and care for the marginalized. As we do, we will see new life rise up all around us.

—Smart Compassion, pp. 126–27

Journal

Reflect on the alignment of your commitments with your values. Where is there misalignment? What are some ways that an eternal perspective might change some practical decisions?

Go Deeper

▸ Take the Gifts Assessment via the QR code.

▸ Identify the decisions and practices that will bring greater alignment between your beliefs and actions. Ask a trusted mentor or friend to pray for you and hold you accountable to those decisions.

Session 6

To What End?

▶ Start waging peace

Pray

Share prayer concerns and praises from the past week and anxiety or excitement about what lies ahead for your group or for you as an individual.

Then pray this prayer together:

Father, we release to you our desires, our past successes and failures, and our expectations for the future. Not our will, but yours be done. Bless us with the wisdom and courage to calibrate our yeses and nos according to your Word. May your grace overflow into all our relationships. Amen.

Ask

Where might God be calling you to step out in greater faith right now? What visions are you pondering in your heart?

If possible, read chapter 12 of *Smart Compassion* before this session.

Begin

"Move fast and break things." The motto of a large social media company might work well for software development, but it's not good advice for churches that want to engage with their communities. People aren't things, and compassion refuses to relate to people primarily as the object of ambition. In the work of collective empowerment, we need to instead move compassionately and restore things.

So what things might God be calling you to restore? Our focus in this last session is to share where we sense God doing a new thing in our lives and how we plan to respond. We will look at the cross as the "first destination and continual centering point for our faith journey with God" (*Smart Compassion*, 159) and will consider how Jacob's journey in Genesis 32 might serve as a model for us.

This last session can also include some conversation on how your individual and collective strategies for community engagement might change. It can also include some brainstorming on takeaways from part 3 of *Smart Compassion*, the collective empowerment section. How will your group put into practice what you have been learning and sensing from God through these weeks of study and discussion?

Read Scripture

Genesis 32:22-30

That night Jacob got up and took his two wives, his two female servants and his eleven sons and crossed the ford of the Jabbok. After he had sent them across the stream, he sent over all his possessions. So Jacob was left alone, and a man wrestled with him till daybreak. When the man saw that he could not overpower him, he touched the socket of Jacob's hip so that his hip was wrenched as he wrestled with the man. Then the man said, "Let me go, for it is daybreak."

But Jacob replied, "I will not let you go unless you bless me."

The man asked him, "What is your name?"

"Jacob," he answered.

Then the man said, "Your name will no longer be Jacob, but Israel, because you have struggled with God and with humans and have overcome."

Jacob said, "Please tell me your name."

But he replied, "Why do you ask my name?" Then he blessed him there.

So Jacob called the place Peniel, saying, "It is because I saw God face to face, and yet my life was spared."

Study

In this story, Jacob came to the end of himself. It's God's desire to get us to this very place where we come to the end of ourselves. It's always a fight. Our name, the titles that define us, our track records, our desires and dreams for the future: all of it comes to the surface with this question: "Who are you?"

Faith journeys in the Old Testament often pass through a threshold, such as a river or cave, where one's sense of identity changes. For Jacob, the Jabbok River served as the turning point. For Elijah and David, the turning point was a cave. In the Old Testament, the cave is often a place of last resort: a gathering place for the disillusioned. When life derails and you're unsure what to trust, where to go, and what really matters, you are entering a cave ordeal. When core theological and identity questions are frightfully blurry, you are entering a cave ordeal. Such places are also where God does some of his best work. Cave experiences can give birth to all sorts of new life.

By becoming a good student of faith journeys, we learn to expect cave ordeals and recognize them as places of both dismantling and rebirth. We learn to see them as transitions rather than destinations and to allow the Lord to excavate our souls, focus our eyes on him, and attend carefully to his voice. A good litmus test for how well we navigate a cave ordeal is how it changes our vision—specifically, what emerges as big and little in our eyes. When our view of God is diminished and people and circumstances loom large, fears and lesser dreams will take hold. Author and pastor John Ortberg describes these lesser dreams as "shadow missions," which aren't full-scale rebellions but rather a partial veering away from commitments. When we recognize God's sovereignty and fix our eyes on him, the same people and circumstances diminish in size and the fears and lesser dreams fail to hook us.

—Smart Compassion, p. 163

Discuss

▸ What is the role of suffering in our faith journeys with God? How does the New Testament teach us to view and respond to such suffering? (See, for example, Romans 5:3-5; Matthew 5:11; Philippians 2:1-11; and John 13.)

▸ Where do you most sense the need for greater alignment of your will with God's Word?

▸ As you look at your gifts, stage of life, sense of calling, and the community's needs, where do you feel led to get involved?

▸ What are some ways you can strengthen relationships within your local community?

▸ Are there any implications from your reading of the DOOR model of collective empowerment? (See pp. 135–58 in *Smart Compassion*.)

> **D**efine a geography and know it.
> **O**bserve what works and implement it.
> **O**perate with measurements and adapt where necessary.
> **R**adiate the vision and empower others.

Journal

The cross of Christ draws us to the core questions of life stewardship. Reflect on if and how you hear and obey God's voice. Consider whether your yeses and nos are aligned with God's yeses and nos.

Go Deeper

▸ Identify some next steps for yourself and the group.

▸ Check out the resources on community mapping via the QR code. Establish a small group to start the process in your community.

▸ Ask some trusted mentors or friends (or both) to intercede for you on the questions and decisions you're pondering.

Where Do We Go from Here?

Let's return to the opening questions of the study. What do you see? What do you sense God doing in this season? What role are you to play in God's story?

Here are a few potential avenues to explore:

1. Continue your study and work together with the "Roadmap for Community Engagement." (See refuge.life website for more information.) The roadmap offers a more detailed process for community engagement that builds on the principles of *Smart Compassion*.

2. Identify potential intersections where your gifting/calling meets with community opportunities/needs. Building on personal and collective spiritual discernment, personal gifts assessment, and community needs assessment, select an area for deeper engagement in your community.

3. Conduct a broader community mapping exercise. After watching the video "Mapping Your Community" available from the QR code, conduct an assessment of your community's health, including child welfare, education, health, housing and transportation, and economic development.

4. Transition to another study on a different facet of community engagement.

Resources

Giving postures: Session 2

What is the relational posture of your approach to service as a church? As a family? As an individual? This diagram outlines five postures of service that move from a weak connection with others (indiscriminate aid) to a strong connection (mutual reciprocity). The lowest category (indiscriminate aid) is best avoided. Strategic aid is best viewed in a triage role (for example, when needs are temporary). The top three postures are where the church's greatest potential influence lies. Which posture has characterized how you interact with others? How might acts of service in the first two categories become more relational and empowering?

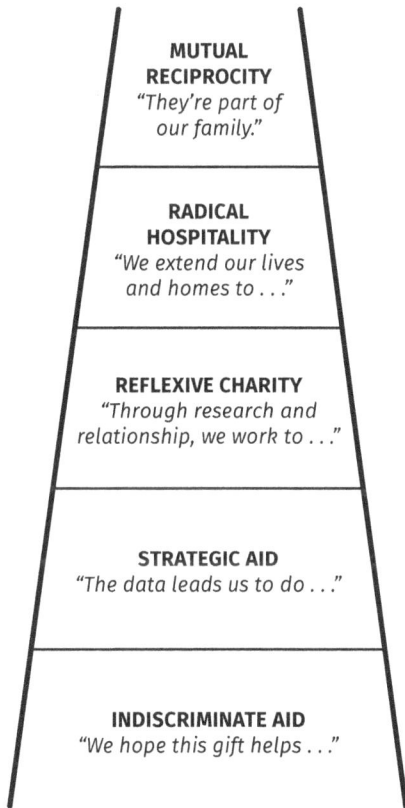

MUTUAL RECIPROCITY
"They're part of our family."

RADICAL HOSPITALITY
"We extend our lives and homes to . . ."

REFLEXIVE CHARITY
"Through research and relationship, we work to . . ."

STRATEGIC AID
"The data leads us to do . . ."

INDISCRIMINATE AID
"We hope this gift helps . . ."

Ways to approach evangelism and justice: Session 3

Congregations blend justice and evangelism in a variety of ways. This spectrum represents the span of approaches congregations can take with regard to evangelism and justice.

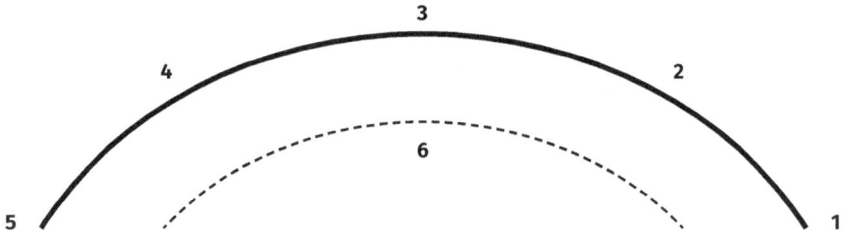

1. EVANGELISM. Individual conversion is the driving pursuit. Repentance of sins, worship, prayer, and personal evangelism are emphasized. Identity, habits, and community stand in clear contrast to those of the world.

2. EVANGELISM > JUSTICE. Individual conversion is supported with outreach. Outreach isn't intended to change the world but rather to draw people to God and ease unnecessary suffering. Emphasis placed on personal transformation through Jesus. There is a clear contrast between God's kingdom and the world.

3. EVANGELISM & JUSTICE. A vision of God's kingdom unites evangelism and justice in a Spirit-driven, Jesus-centered view of life. Emphasis placed on personal and collective transformation through Jesus so that the gospel will spread and God's kingdom will transform the world. A clear contrast between God's kingdom and the world is maintained.

4. JUSTICE > EVANGELISM. Justice is supported with evangelism. Solidarity with the world is emphasized, but there is a desire to retain good aspects of conservative models. Evangelism is more a means to an end than a desire to see people experience God's salvation.

5. JUSTICE. Social justice is the driving pursuit. Solidarity with and improvement of the world are emphasized. Identity, habits, and community reinforce positive connections with the world. Conservative religious practices and spiritual zeal are deemphasized.

6. UNITY > JUSTICE & EVANGELISM. Interpersonal peace is the driving pursuit. Emphasis is placed on keeping opposing groups together and drawing out the strengths of each while minimizing differences. Identity, habits, and community reinforce the need for cohesiveness within the community.

Online Tools

The following resources are grouped into two categories: tools for community mapping, and models and strategies for community engagement. Additional resources can be found at refuge.life.

Tools for community mapping

Child welfare

▶ View a primary source for federal, state, and local data on child and family well-being: http://datacenter.kidscount.org/.

▶ Map the geography of opportunity for children in the hundred largest metropolitan areas in the United States: http://www.diversitydatakids.org/data/childopportunitymap.

▶ Map the federal funds coming to your area and evaluate programs: http://youth.gov/.

▶ See state-by-state policy information on a variety of child welfare topics: https://www.childtrends.org/research/state/.

▶ Become familiar with hundreds of measures of child well-being and policy analysis: http://www.diversitydatakids.org/.

▶ Find case-level information on all children in foster care and those who have been adopted: http://www.acf.hhs.gov/cb/research-data-technology/statistics-research/afcars.

Health

▶ See a primary resource for county health data: http://www.countyhealthrankings.org/.

▶ Find treatment centers: https://findtreatment.samhsa.gov/.

▶ Explore the CDC's portal for health statistics: https://www.cdc.gov/nchs/.

▶ Use this interactive data tool to explore data and technical information related to the Healthy People 2020 objectives: https://www.healthypeople.gov/.

▶ Find out more about the glaring variations in how medical resources are distributed and used in the United States: http://www.dartmouthatlas.org/.

Economic development

▶ Use this budget-based measure of the real cost of living and an alternative to the federal poverty measure by state: http://www.selfsufficiencystandard.org/.

▶ Calculate a family's income at different earnings levels, considering the effects of payroll taxes, income taxes, tax credits, childcare expenses, and cash and in-kind benefits according to current federal and state policies: http://nicc.urban.org/netincomecalculator/.

▶ Estimate the cost of living in your community or region: http://livingwage.mit.edu/.

▶ See a snapshot of local economic indicators: http://economic-toolbox.mit.edu/.

▶ Discover youth programs with strong evidence for success: http://www.blueprintsprograms.com/.

▶ Map the meal gap: http://map.feedingamerica.org/county/2014/overall.

Housing and transportation

▶ Map the rental housing crisis in the United States: http://apps.urban.org/features/rental-housing-crisis-map/.

▶ See the Census Bureau's updated estimates of income and poverty statistics: https://www.census.gov/did/www/saipe/.

▶ View information metrics from the CHAS (Comprehensive Housing Affordability Strategy) data set: https://www.huduser.gov/portal/datasets/cp/CHAS/data_querytool_chas.html.

▶ See a housing and transportation cost index: http://htaindex.cnt.org/.

▶ View your city's or neighborhood's "walk score," which measures walkability: https://www.walkscore.com.

Education

▶ View a primary source for federal, state, and local data on child and family well-being: http://datacenter.kidscount.org/.
▶ Learn about evidence-based educational support programs: http://www.blueprintsprograms.com/.
▶ Find school information and parenting resources: http://www.greatschools.org/.

GIS (geographic information system) platforms

▶ Discover a free and open-source GIS platform: http://www.qgis.org/en/site/.
▶ Learn more about a complete, cloud-based mapping platform: https://www.arcgis.com/features/index.html.
▶ Investigate an easy-to-use online mapping device with accessible data: https://www.policymap.com/.

Additional tools

▶ Use a free online survey software and questionnaire tool: https://www.surveymonkey.com/.
▶ Learn more about a primary search tool for census-related data: https://factfinder.census.gov/faces/nav/jsf/pages/index.xhtml.
▶ Discover a data analysis and extraction tool: https://dataferrett.census.gov/.

Models and strategies for community engagement

▶ Find a review of many evidence-based programs related to youth development: http://www.blueprintsprograms.com/.
▶ Discover a structured form of collaboration to address a specific social problem: https://ssir.org/articles/entry/collective_impact.
▶ Find program examples of collective impact principles: http://www.promiseneighborhoodsinstitute.org/ and http://www.communitiesthatcare.net/.
▶ See refuge.life for more examples of models and strategies for community engagement.